My Greatest Loss Turned into a Purposeful WIN

Brandi J-E McAlister, MS, CSC, CLC

ISBN: 979-8-9864642-8-2

Printed in the United States of America

Email address: praytheimpossible@gmail.com

Website: www.praytheimpossible.com

Cover photo credit Mr. Brian Johnson Photography

Disclaimer: This book is the author's personal, non-fictional story. Every account in the book is true, and the events are portrayed to the best of the author's memory. While all the stories in this book are true, names and identifying details were eliminated to protect the privacy of the people involved. The author does not assume and hereby disclaims any liability to any party for any loss, damage, emotional distress, or disruption as a result of the book content.

Any internet addresses, books, products, blogs are offered as a resource and not intended in any way to imply an endorsement by BFF Publishing House.

In loving memory of my father, AKA Boo

I dedicate my third book solely to you. You were Pray the Impossible's top supporter. I can hear your voice now saying, "Girllll, you just don't know how powerful you are." You were right. I didn't know how powerful I was until I began reflecting on my journey after December 3, 2021. Writing this book has shown me the power of God that lives within me. Although you're not physically here, you will live in my heart, through my story and my God-given purpose on earth.

Love Always,

Your Boo

TABLE OF CONTENTS

PREFACE

What is grief? Deep sorrow, especially caused by someone's death.

Grieve: to feel or express great sadness, especially when someone dies.

Mourn: to feel or show deep sorrow or regret for; feel regret or sadness about the loss or disappearance of something.

I was never taught what grief is or how one should properly grieve. I can recall a time when family members on my father's side were passing away what seemed to be every two years from 1992 to 2005. As a child, I remember not going to school for the whole week and going to my great grandparents' house with the entire family, and then, once everything was said and done, everyone went back to their regular scheduled programming. It felt as if the duration of the grieving process was the week that took place when the family member passed until the funeral services. Once the services were over, the grieving stopped. Or did it really stop? Perhaps I wasn't aware of the internal pain that remained when the casket went six feet into the ground. Or, perhaps, arguments and excessive drinking around the holidays to mask the pain was a form of grieving that I thought was "normal."

Death is certain. How a loved one transitions, however, is never certain. It can be sudden, where you may not have a chance to say goodbye. It can be predicted based on a disease or illness, where you can begin to prepare and are able to say your last goodbye. It can be tragic, leaving you angry, shattered, and paralyzed in pain. It can be long and drawn out, where you watch your loved one deteriorate and suffer in front of you. Either way, death has a sting that is painful and leaves an impact that changes the rest of your life.

What does grief look and feel like?

» Isolation
» Smiling while crying on the inside
» Denial
» State of shock
» Disbelief
» Depression
» Substance abuse to mask the pain
» Anger
» Heartbreak
» Devastation
» Anxiety
» Tightness in your chest
» Feeling triggered by memories of your loved one
» Silence

- Being unable to function and perform daily tasks
- Finding ways to honor your loved one
- Reminiscing
- Living with guilt and regret
- Reliving the day you lost your loved one
- Yelling
- Spiraling out of control
- Seeking therapy or counseling
- Suppressing feelings
- Experiencing waves of mixed emotions
- Pressing through
- Paralysis
- Not knowing what to do or how to live without your loved one
- Feeling overcome with deep sadness
- Being unable to control emotions
- Shutting down
- Busyness
- Avoidance
- Excessive sleeping or lack of sleep
- Immobilization

I'd experienced loss before—loss of relationships that I thought were for a lifetime, laid off from jobs that I thought were secure—but this time, I was about to lose a piece of myself that I worked hard to become, and a piece of myself that I would never see again. I thought 2021 was my winning year. I even changed it to say "Twenty Twenty WON." Boy, was I in for a ride that I didn't see coming. Since being laid off in 2020, I knew unemployment was eventually going to come to an end. I decided that I would move back home with my mom to save money and pay off debt, and then start to look for a new place. My lease was ending in March. I had a plan, but God also had a plan.

I told my dad about my plans, and he said that he would come up from South Carolina to help me move. After all, he had made friends in the complex over the eight years of me living there; he insisted on coming back to tell them goodbye. But he made a comment that I brushed off. He said, "Yeah, I'm going to come up there because this may be my last trip up there." I paid him no attention. I thought he was just talking as usual. In 2019, after the death of his last sibling, he started to make comments about himself being next. He fell into a depression because his mother, father, sister, and two brothers preceded him in death. I didn't know that he was still grieving three years later. I assumed that he'd "moved on." But now, I understand that you cannot put a time limit on grief, nor can you rush someone's grieving process. He would tell me that he didn't have any family, and I would assure him that yes, he did. He had my brother, my niece, and me. Now, I understood I was a part of the family he created. He was talking about the family that he originally belonged to. I told him that it was time for him to move back up to New Jersey. I told him his time was up in South Carolina after living there for 16 years. He agreed that he would come once I found him a 55-and-up community to reside in.

It was now March 2021, and he came up to help me move. I noticed how he didn't really help me move. He could barely lift a box, and I was doing all the work! I thought my dad was being my dad by wanting to be in the mix, have a sense of control, and oversee what was going on. He was moving a little slower and was looking thinner, but I had charged it to him being depressed and not eating. But I had gotten used to him being smaller since that had become his frame over the past three years. April, May, and June were my winning seasons. I was traveling, living my best life, and in a good space. In July, I contracted COVID, and that was the beginning of the turning point in my Twenty Twenty WON. By the time August came around, I was praying and expecting a new beginning. I was feeling better, but it seemed like God had gone silent on me. I tried everything I knew how to do, and it seemed like God was not moved. Things were looking bleak, and I became angry. I couldn't understand how things just seemed to not be working in my favor. Once again, I felt that I was doing my best, doing the Lord's work, and supporting others. But what about me, God? I felt spiritually disconnected from God and was going through the motions at this point.

In the midst of my personal defeat, I was thriving in my businesses. I was in the process of planning my first fundraiser event for my nonprofit, Blessed by Brandi, Inc. My dad was a huge supporter, and when I told him about the event, he went back and forth about deciding if he was going to attend. Then, one day, he called me and said, "Eh, I guess I'll come. This may be my last event." Once again, I brushed him off. He'd said something similar to this in March, and he was still here.

By the end of August, a part-time job opportunity presented itself that I knew for sure was a win. I had plans, but God had plans that I knew nothing about. On September 5, my unemployment came to an end. On September 6, the promising job opportunity was no longer an opportunity, and just when I felt like I was losing in life and losing myself that year, the greatest loss was about to show up. September 7, my dad left SC to come to New Jersey. He would usually call me during his train rides to let me know when he made it to Washington, DC; Philly; and Trenton, but this train ride was different. He didn't call me. He was scheduled to arrive at Newark Penn Station around 11:55 p.m. I kept calling his phone, and it was going straight to voicemail. I was beginning to get worried because I realized he didn't call me to tell me he was on the train headed up to New Jersey. I arrived a little after midnight on the 8th. I called his phone several times, and he finally answered. I was so frustrated with him that I started yelling at him. I was asking him where he was, and he was at a part of the train station where I didn't usually pick him up from. His voice was different, but I charged it to him having a few drinks. One last time, I asked where he was, and he responded, "Brandi, I can't walk." I asked, "What do you mean, you 'can't walk'?" After about 15 minutes, he finally made his way to the loading zone where my car was parked. I saw him from a distance, and he just stopped. I honked my horn, but he wouldn't move.

A stranger saw me trying to get my dad's attention, and he asked me who I was looking for. I told him I was looking for my dad and pointed to where he was standing. The man asked me what my father's name was, and I said Barry. He began to yell, "Barry, your daughter is here!" But I noticed my father was leaning against the pillar and unable to move. The kind man went over to meet my father and helped him walk to my car. I had never seen my father in this state before. He could barely walk. I was confused at what I was witnessing because just a few weeks ago, he sounded as if everything was fine. The man put my father in my car. My father fastened his seat belt and held onto the seat belt for dear life. I noticed something was different. Something was missing. My father only had two plastic bags filled with his snacks. He did not have any luggage. I asked him where his luggage was, and in a soft-spoken voice, he said, "I didn't have time to go to the laundromat." I put his two plastic bags in my back seat, and the first thought that came to mind was, *Did he come here to die?* I drove us home trying to hold back tears.

When we arrived at my mother's house, I was able to truly see him in his current state. A state of shock and confusion came upon me. What was going on? I went into the bathroom, shed some tears, and prayed to God that he wouldn't pass over the weekend. I had been planning an event that he purposely came up for. Immediately, I asked God to give my father weeks on earth.

Over the next few days, he was not himself. He barely ate, and he watched TV and slept a lot. That was not his usual routine. I remember that, a few days later, he finally drank some water. I shared with my mother that he told me he was dehydrated. My mother said, "That's not dehydration." She insisted that he go to the emergency room, but he refused and said he was fine. I received a phone call from my father's friend who had dropped him off at the train station in SC. He told me my father had given him my phone number. His friend was calling to check on him. He told me, "I don't know how he made it on the train for 14 hours. He was in so much pain. I didn't think he was going to make it." Reality still hadn't set in. *When did this drastic change occur? When and how did I miss this? How didn't I know he was in this much pain?* September 12 was the day of my Kentucky Derby Fundraising Event. My mother asked my father if he was going to attend. He told her no at first, then later changed his mind. When I arrived at the venue to set up, I noticed my friend's mother was putting a pain relief patch on his back. He was so tired and in pain. I asked him if he wanted to sit in my car while I set up, and he insisted that he was fine at the table. Moments later, he changed his mind and took me up on my offer. I handed him my keys, and he began to walk himself to the car. Moments later, I turned around and saw him on all fours in the grass. My sister from another mister and I rushed over to help him. We picked him up and walked him to my car. After getting him in my car, she asked me, "Do you think it's cancer?" I looked at her with tears welling in my eyes and said, "I don't know." I immediately had to shake the thought and feelings off because in less than two hours, I was going to have a venue filled with guests, and I had to be at my best to host. He spent the majority of the event sleeping in a private room in the venue. People checked on him throughout the event to make sure he was OK. Only a select group of people knew what I was dealing with while I smiled and carried myself in a way where no one would know what I was going through. Towards the end of the event, my father came outside, sat on the steps, and looked in awe from a distance at the event that he persevered through pain to attend. At the end of the night, he decided to go to the ER the next day after being convinced by many people.

On September 13, we got ourselves ready to go to the ER. Mentally, I prepared myself to drop him off, then come back and get him in a few hours. I took him to McDonald's to put something in his stomach, and we made our way. I spent 12 hours in the ER with him. We found out that his blood pressure was low, his magnesium level was low, his potassium level was low, and he was dehydrated. The doctors performed X-rays on him. They were going to release him—until the X-rays showed that he had either pneumonia or cancer in his lungs. Hours later, they had to run a CT scan. The CT scan came back that he had stage 4 lung cancer. His response as he laid on the gurney in the ER hallway was, "I knew it. This is why I didn't want to come here." I was numb. I couldn't believe what I had just heard. I cried my eyes out. Next, I accepted what the doctors told me. After all, he'd been smoking since he was 13 years old. Lung cancer wasn't too far-fetched. But it was now time to make plans to officially move him back to New Jersey and figure out what his treatment options were.

The next 83 days were filled with a wave of emotions, stress, frustration, exhaustion, operating on autopilot, accepting life without him, praying to God to heal his body, shutting down, grieving without knowing I was grieving, trying to ask the doctors the right questions, keeping his friends and family updated, taking notes from all the different doctors that were calling me, having hard conversations that most people like to avoid, and watching my father deteriorate and suffer before my eyes.

December 3, 2021 was a day I could have never prepared for. It was a day I never thought would have been my experience. I had always prepared myself to get a phone call from someone in South Carolina informing me that my dad had passed. I mentally prepared myself to go to South Carolina to identify him and have his remains sent back to New Jersey. I could have never been so wrong in my life. That morning, I read my Advent devotional plan in the Bible app. It posed the question, "Is there someone you need to communicate with more clearly?" I journaled, "God, I need to praise and worship You more and be more vocal." The scripture for the plan was Lamentations 3:4: "He has made my skin and flesh grow old. He has broken my bones. He has besieged and surrounded me with anguish and distress." While meditating on the word, I thought about Papa. I went back to my journal and wrote down, "I'm going to communicate more with Papa and tell him how I feel instead of staring at him and asking him how he feels. I'm going to tell him I love him more today." Next, I did my usual routine; I went into the living room to check on him and make sure he was OK.

His phone rang, and it was the chaplain from hospice asking if he could pray for him. I told him that he was sleeping, and he said it was OK that He could still pray for him. He asked me what time was good for him to come to the house, and I told him around 12 p.m. A few minutes later, my father's minister called. That day, he was led to go down the road to my father's cousin's house to get my father's phone number. He heard my father was ill, but he was not aware of how serious it was. I answered the phone and told my father that his minister was on the phone. They chatted briefly, and then my father told him he was tired and that he had to go to sleep.

It was very strange—or was it?—for the chaplain and my father's minister to call back to back. At the moment, I did not think anything of it. I had a meeting from 11 a.m. until 12 p.m. When the meeting ended, my life as I once knew it was about to change forever. It was quiet, and then I heard him make a loud groan. I came into the living room and asked if he was OK. He said that he needed to go to the bathroom. I tried to assist him to his commode, but his body was dead weight. I then tried to pass him his urinal, but excruciating pain had come over him. For the next hour, I watched him fight, kick, scream, release bodily fluids, and begin his transition process. The interesting part is that my spirit knew he was transitioning. I had never witnessed a person transition, but I knew he was. My mother was running errands that day and called me in the midst. Crying hysterically, I told her that he was transitioning, and she was going to get home as soon as she could.

It was now past 12 p.m., and the chaplain hadn't shown up yet. Although I'm the Spiritual Friendvisor of Pray the Impossible, at that moment, I was Brandi, Barry's daughter. I needed someone to pray because I didn't have the strength to do so. I called my good girlfriend, who is my spiritual sister, and I will never forget what she did for me and my father in that moment I will never forget. She witnessed what I was witnessing and prayed over him. She then said she was on her way to my house because she knew I was still home alone. As he continued to fight, I told him that I loved him, and he told me that he loved me, too. I told him that he didn't have to fight anymore.

His last audible words were, "Lord, I'm coming." Two hours later, the house was filled with the nurse, my mom, my two friends, my aunt, and my cousin. By this time, the nurse cleaned him up, he was administered morphine to reduce the pain, and he was given oxygen to help with his breathing. For the next two hours, I was having an out-of-body experience—trying to process what I was witnessing, trying to keep my mind off things, not fully understanding what was going on, making numerous phone calls to let his friends and family members say their last goodbyes, and in disbelief of what would possibly happen next. The chaplain finally arrived and prayed over him. We played gospel music to set the atmosphere. After a while, I decided to change the music so that he could hear the songs that he loved. As Isaac Hayes's "By the Time I get to Phoenix" was playing, my friend noticed my father's breathing was beginning to change. She said, "Bran, you may want to go by your dad. His breathing is changing." I hopped off the couch and climbed on the futon with my dad. I held his hand and laid on his chest. When the lyrics, "By the time I get to Phoenix, she'll be rising," came on, I noticed his breathing was becoming more faint. Around 4:10 p.m., I watched him take his last breath. I sat there in disbelief of what I never imagined I would witness. I laid on his chest, cried out, and asked him why he didn't say bye. In his last moments of life, God allowed me to give my father what he needed, which was my love and affection. In return, I was able to tap into the little girl inside of me who loved her daddy. My spirit was pleased to have shared that special moment with him that I will cherish for the rest of my life. Following that, a sense of peace came over me that I had never felt in my entire life. God had given me His perfect peace that surpassed all understanding.

On December 26, 2021, I wrote:

"202WON

We made it to the last Sunday in this year, so that means we WON against every test, trial, and tribulation that was sent against us. We may have tested positive for COVID, may have experienced financial difficulties, may have not received the very one thing you've been believing in God for this year, but you WON if you're still here.

If you still have your faith, still have a praise on your tongue, still have a worship in your spirit, you have already WON. Regardless of what you may have thought was sent to come against you, God turned it around for your good, exceeded your expectations in certain situations, blessed you with more than you thought He would, and worked things out in your favor that you knew nothing about. In the end, you actually WON. Reflect on the course of the year and how you've WON because you're still here."

December 31, 2021:

"Twenty Twenty WON

I can remember the MAJOR Ls I took this year, but you would never know it because I took them with the grace of God. This year, God made me unusually and supernaturally strong. This year,

I trusted God in ways I never thought I would. I made peace with what God decided for my life this year.

As I reflect on these Ls, I understand that they prepared me for December 3, 2021 at 4:07 p.m. I experienced my biggest loss four weeks ago today, but come to find out it was my biggest win.

Listen, Barry Sr. is my forever ANGEL! You already know he didn't play about me while he was here on earth, so you know he's in Heaven ready to intervene and turn this muthafckr UP down here on earth on my behalf! That brings me comfort and peace because nobody plays with his daughter.

My good days outweigh my bad days because as I look through my photos and videos of this year, I smile and laugh and remember those were my best days and memories.

2021 still did right by me because I was able to travel; overcame and survived COVID; was able to keep my faith and peace; was successful in my business; was able to hold my daddy's hand and lay on his chest as he took his last breath; and received an OVERFLOW OF LOVE, unexpected blessings, and support from my family, friends, and those I'd never expect!

But the real win is that I made it to December 31, 2021! With that being said, I WON. I saw a post that said, "This year, God made you strong; next year He's going to make you happy."

God, I'm holding you to that. ~ Brandi"

Initially, I interpreted my 2021 experiences as my greatest loss. But as I reflected over the course of my year, I saw how God turned my greatest loss into a purposeful win. The win is that I'm able to share my personal experience with you to encourage you on your own journey of grief and loss. My win is that I'm able to shed light on finding purpose in the loss and allowing it to become a purposeful win. My win is that even in the midst of a devastating loss, I found strength that I never knew God had already equipped me with. My win is that I saw God move in my life in a way I had never experienced.

Introduction

What you're about to read is a heartfelt entry I wrote for my dad a few days after he passed, which I shared with the attendees at my father's memorial service. This was not his eulogy; this was Barry's daughter expressing from her heart the good, bad, and indifferent times she encountered with him. As I reflected over the past, it brought me a sense of comfort and peace. It made my heart smile, and I wanted to share it with the world. In the moments of reflection, God showed up and gave me insight and revelation as to the points in life when He showed up and how He caused all those memories to work together for the good because I love Him and am called according to His purpose.

12/12/21 John Barry McAlister's Service

God Is Able to Do Anything

GEMS (God Enthused Messages Spoken) from My Heart

Thursday nights at 8:00 p.m., my dad would tune in to my Instagram live show and would often comment, "Hey, Boo; it's

Papa," or "Papa loves you." It's only right that I have a heart-to-heart with him today.

Here are some GEMS from my heart that I learned throughout this process and his last days here.

God is able to give you more than you ask for, pray for, or even imagined.

I picked you up from Newark Penn Station on September 7. I recalled the scripture, "God will add days to your life." I asked God to give me weeks. I didn't want you to go the weekend of my event. God gave me 87 days, or 12 weeks.

God is able to transform your heart.

My dad loved in a way that he knew how. It may have been aggressive, but he loved. I wasn't affectionate towards him as a child and into adulthood. He would always say, "I love you," or, "Daddy loves you," and I'd respond, "Yeah, yeah," or, "OK." Or, I wouldn't respond at all, and I'd say, "Talk to you later." During his days in the hospital or in the rehabilitation center, I started initiating it, and then he'd look at me. I would say, "Boo, you didn't say it back," and then he'd say, "I love you, too." December 3, 2021, I was journaling after reading the Advent reading plan. It posed the question, "Is there someone you need to communicate with more clearly?" I wrote, "God I need to praise and worship You more and be more vocal." When I read Lamentations 3:4, "He has made my skin and flesh grow old. He has broken my bones. He has besieged and surrounded me with anguish and distress," I thought about Papa. I went back and wrote down, "I'm going to communicate more with Papa and tell him how I feel instead of staring at him and asking him how he feels. I'm going to tell him I love him more today." Around 12:15 p.m., when he began to transition, I told him I loved him. He told me he loved me, too. Then, as he was taking his last breath, I got on the futon, held his hand, and laid on his chest as he took his final breath. God transformed my heart, and I gave my father something I'd never given him before: my love from a heart that has God's love in it.

God is able to redeem you.

My father was far from perfect. He made a lot of mistakes, but he knew God. He may have strayed at times, he may not have applied God's word to his life, but he knew God, and God knew him. I had a conversation with his minister, Brother Tillman, in the midst of his transition, and he shared with me that before my father left South Carolina to visit New Jersey, he repented for his sins.

God is able to give you the strength to forgive.

In 2019, I finally accepted my father for who he was. He wasn't perfect, and that's who God used as the vessel to bring me into this world. I used to say, "Why can't he just be normal?". But how he was raised and what he struggled with as a child made and shaped him. Once I accepted and understood he was fighting his own battles, I had to forgive, realize, and apply, "Honor thy mother and father." No matter how much I disliked his actions and behaviors at times, I still had to respect him as my father.

God is able to restore anything, anyone, and any relationship.

On December 25, 2000, our family broke up. God used the passing of my Uncle Robert to restore our family in 2019. November 26, 2020 was the first Thanksgiving we (my mom, brother, father, and myself) spent as a family.

God is able to complete the work He began.

On November 12, 2021, after the doctors said my father could possibly have two to six months left with us, he responded, "As long as I get to see grandbaby." On November 25, 2021, God completed the work, and Ryleigh spent Thanksgiving with us. On November 27, 2021, the five of us took what would be our last family photo with my father here.

God is able to make the good days outweigh the bad days.

In his last days, I remember he was spicy, moody, and snappy. In the hospital and rehab, I remember he was feisty, so I took a day off from him. The next day, he asked, "What were you doing yesterday?" Or, if I was late, he'd ask, "What you been doing all day?" I'd respond, "Sir," and laugh. I can recall the "bad times" we had—the arguments, our father-daughter fights—but Sunday, as I was going through photos, I immediately remembered the good times and memories. Our good days outweigh our bad days and bad memories. I now laugh at the bad days and memories.

God is able to do anything. What I once thought was impossible, God made possible. I love you, Boo!

This is my personal journey of losing a loved one and how I learned to process grief and mourning. God placed God Enthused Messages Spoken from My Heart within me to share with you to bring comfort and encouragement on your journey. Everyone's grief process looks and feels different and should not be compared to another. The only similarities we share is that God promises that He will be with us. As we grow closer to Him, He will reveal Himself more and in new ways.

Let my story be used as a testament of God's faithfulness in spite of what you are currently going through. I pray that through my story, you can see how God showed up, and that if He did it for me, He will show up in the way you need Him to.

Chapter 1

God Is in You

On October 21, 2021, I posted on Pray the Impossible, "God in You. When God is in you, He will use you to bring comfort to those who are weeping with sorrow, grieving, and hurting. They may not be strong enough to call on God themselves, but the God in you will provide words of encouragement that will strengthen them. The God in you has the power to encourage with your words."

WOW! I cannot believe that God led me to write that less than two months before my father died. I guess those words were meant for me now. Here I am, sharing with you how to turn what you consider your greatest loss into a purposeful win.

The first year after my father's passing was an emotional roller coaster. I know seven people who lost their father, one person who lost their godfather, three people who lost their mother, one person who passed away, one person who lost his wife and then his daughter later in the year, one person who lost her husband, one person who lost their nephew, one person who had a miscarriage, and another person who lost their brother. These are just people who I personally know, and my spirit was heavily grieving. There were moments in the beginning of my grieving process when it was as if I was reliving the passing of my father. There were moments when I didn't have the strength to send condolences. There were moments when I was numb and became immobile. There were moments when I was able to muster up strength to pour into those because of the amount of people who were loving on me, pouring into me, praying for me, and supporting me.

Although I was grieving and mourning, I still had an assignment that needed to be fulfilled. I had to stay on top of my posts on Pray the Impossible and Blessed by Brandi, Inc. and encourage, inspire, and motivate people on a daily basis, even through my tears, grief, and mourning. Little did I know that God was equipping me for something that would lead me to a greater purpose in life.

December 13, 2021: The day after we celebrated my father's life, I received an email that my Big Sister from my sorority had passed. This was the sorority sister who called me to ask if I was still interested in becoming a Delta. This was the same sorority sister who had vouched for me to become a part of this illustrious sorority. I had felt obligated to attend her funeral out of respect. Although it was possibly too soon, in my heart, I had to pay my respects.

January 1, 2022: I got a call from my brother. He was crying, grieving, in pain, and beginning to spiral because of the loss of our father. I had to be his support and suppress my grieving and mourning to talk him off the ledge. It was extremely heavy.

January 2, 2022: I received a phone call from my sorority sister and friend asking me to pray for her mother because she went into cardiac arrest. All I could do was let God use me to pray with a broken heart for someone who did not have the strength to pray for herself.

January 7, 2022: The same sorority sister and friend who had called asking for prayer flew up from Atlanta to New York to see her mother. She had asked me to come over to do her daughter's hair. While there, she received a phone call that her mother was now brain-dead. She felt horrible that I was there while she received the call, and in no way, form, or fashion did she want me to be triggered. In that moment, on the sixth Friday after my father's passing, around the same time he took his last breath, I offered words of encouragement as I had just lost my father.

March 18 to 19, 2022: I was a guest speaker for a two-day women's event called The Cleansing in Stockbridge, Georgia. I was tasked with speaking to a room full of women who were broken, hurting, and grieving about becoming new. How could I encourage women about becoming new while I was in the process of becoming new?

June 16, 2022: I got a call from my friend in the middle of the night asking me to pray for her. Her aunt was rushed to the hospital, and things were not looking good. With anxiety rushing through my body, reliving the moment when I had to make that phone call to my friend asking for prayer, I prayed to God because she needed strength as she was being strong for her cousin. Within an hour, her aunt passed.

June 22, 2022: The cousin of my friend whose aunt (the cousin's mom) had just passed away texted me that she needed me. We spoke, and she asked me to preach at her mother's funeral. She wanted to incorporate me in her mother's service because her mother had heard my prayer at my friend's 35th birthday party six months prior.

June 26, 2022: My brother FaceTimed me after he had gotten into a car accident. If you had seen his car, you would have thought, *How did he survive that?* There was no one but God and my father watching over him.

June 29, 2022: The day after my father's birthday, I prayed for my friend, her cousin, and their family at their aunt's/mother's funeral. I remembered sitting in the first row just six months prior, and I remembered the amount of people who prayed for me. I had an obligation to pay it forward, to be that support for them as I had received.

Humanly speaking, I do not know how I was able to handle the weight of my grief and everyone's else's grief in the first six months of my new reality. But I remembered God is in me. This is how I decided to turn my greatest loss into a purposeful win. God gave me His strength to do all things. God was using me to be there for those who were not able to find strength to make it through.

Sometimes, when we go through an experience such as the loss of a loved one, we hone in on our feelings, pain, heartache, and heartbreak. But there is going to be someone who will experience the loss of a loved one after you, and God will use you to help them in their time of need. When God is in you, He can use you broken, hurt, and in pain to help lift someone. Even in my grief, being able to pour into them was healing and therapeutic for me.

Chapter 2

Comfort Is On the Way

December 6, 2021, three days after my dad passed, I received a heartfelt message on Instagram from one of my followers:

"Hey, love. You were on my mind this morning. Losing a parent is hard; you never get over that emptiness. From experience, here's what I will say: Your dad got to see the woman you became, and you made him damn proud. And now, he has the ability to see the woman you will grow to become. His love will never erase because of him. Whoever you decide to be with, you will know if it's the real deal because of the love your father has shown and expressed to you.

Your path was already predestined, and I'm a believer without knowing you, your dad, or your relationship with him personally that you're built to spread the goodness of God, all His promises, and all His power in making what people think is impossible brought them closer to God, whether they told you or not.

The load of grief lightens, but never really goes away! Do you know the doors and the divine intervention that is now about to triple because your dad has more power on the other side to continue to guide you along the way? The anointing on your life is not something that just happened. He knew you before He gave you to your parents. I want you to keep your head up and grieve how you must. There's no rush or time frame on it. Walk in your power; He's always with you. His work as a father is not finished; it's only begun. There are big things ahead of you to come. Also, you'll begin to see signs that he's still present. I see favor on you. I see doors about to open for you, and I see that this is a door for another project for you. And it may seem crazy, someone you never met speaking over you like this, but that's OK, LOL. I know my position with God, and sometimes, you gotta be OK with being looked at as crazy, LOL. I'm a woman of faith. I stand firm in my conviction when I tell you that your ministry and all you're going through is NOT for you. You're built differently. You cannot move how the others move. Your calling is different. You've always felt different from others. Tap into that THING CALLED 'DIFFERENT.' Your dad doesn't want you to slow up; he says now is the time to STEP ON THE GAS! You got some things to do, lady!

You got a lot more souls to save, and you and him can tag team it together. You have the gift. You'll begin to see how it heightens in these next few weeks. You'll begin to notice the afflicted before they even mention their struggles, and whoever has been on your mind lately, give them a call. You're stronger than you know."

WOW! This totally blew my mind and comforted me at the same time. I've had people send comforting words, but this stood out the most and spoke to my broken spirit. What stuck out the most during the initial reading was when she informed me that I would begin to see small signs that my father is still present. She was right! After she shared that with me, I began to keep a journal of the times my father showed up. For 365 days, I saw him show up in ways that comforted my spirit, just when I needed him. It was comforting to know that although he was physically gone, he was still with me.

During your loss, God is going to send someone to comfort you, to speak to your broken spirit, and to give you words of hope that will speak to your future.

How did I find ways to comfort myself during the first year of grief?

- » I created a playlist of songs my father played during my childhood and songs that remind me of him. There were days when that was the playlist I listened to.
- » The day he passed, I wore my black Pray the Impossible hoodie and black sweatpants. I wore that same outfit every Friday until it became too warm outside.
- » I kept a daily journal of every time his presence showed up to let me know he's still with me.

- I created a "Favorites" album in my phone with pictures and videos of him that I would watch.
- Saved all his voice messages.
- I ordered three bracelets with his initials, JBM.
- I counted every Friday until his six-month death anniversary on June 3, 2022.
- I would post pictures and videos of him on social media anytime I missed him.
- I was given a cremation heart with my favorite picture of us and a pendant in which I had his ashes placed. I wear the necklace every day.
- I was given angel wings with his picture, and I placed it on my rearview mirror in my car for him to watch over me.
- I put his prayer card from his celebration of life on my dashboard to watch over me.
- Sometimes, I would call his phone to hear his voicemail until the phone provider disconnected his service.
- Every Friday, I would sit in the area of the house where he transitioned.
- I would rewatch the videos I took him during his last hours alive the week he transitioned.
- I created an altar in my room with his urn, obituary, roses from his floral arrangement, and pictures of us.
- I changed my screensaver to his picture.
- I would talk about my dad and his transition experience any chance I'd get.

Chapter 3

You Will Never Be the Same

A great friend of mine shared with me that when you lose a loved one—or, in my case, my father—a piece of you dies with them. He expressed this based on his experience with losing his grandfather who raised him. I must say I agree. The day I watched my father take his last breath, the person I was before 12 p.m. died with him. The person I was before I picked him up at Newark Penn station—I have not seen her since.

The day before, the day of, and the day after you experience a great loss, you will never be the same. After the loss, we try hard to get back to who we were before the trauma, devastation, pain, and heartbreak took place. We have to understand that we will never be that person again. We have a new reality and a new life that we must learn how to navigate without our person. We are new people, and we must navigate through these new feelings.

Going through this new transformation of figuring out the new me led me to tap into areas of my personal life that needed work. Pray the Impossible and Blessed by Brandi, Inc. were thriving, and I was trying to survive.

I met with my Accountability/Business/Life Coach, and he gave me an assignment on February 25, 2022. The assignment was to create a SWOT (Strengths, Weakness, Opportunities, Threats) analysis of my personal life. It was to challenge me to dig deep and think about the personal areas of my life that I have not been thriving and excelling in.

My Strengths: supportive, encouraging, creative, helpful, loving, personable, wise, transparent, influencer, strong, consistent, resilient, energetic, and hard worker.

Although these are great qualities, he helped me to see that these are the qualities I use as an entrepreneur, in my business, as life and spiritual coach, and most importantly, as support to help other people. These strengths were not being applied in my personal life.

My Weaknesses: not expressing true feelings, sweeping situations under the rug to keep peace, not addressing issues right away (non-confrontational), holding on longer than needed, not saying NO, not always open, stubborn at times, and not always asking the right questions.

These weaknesses have always been here throughout the course of my life. Since exploring this new me, it was now time to heal and turn these weaknesses into opportunities. I decided that since I would never be the same, I was going to work on my weaknesses.

I was going to be intentional about addressing issues right away, be open to trying new things, establish healthy boundaries, speak up, and feel all my feelings (sit with them, but not stay in them).

This season of my life was about me protecting my peace. I understood that I was in a very fragile state with grief, working on my weaknesses, and learning the new person I became. I no longer have the patience, capacity, or energy I had prior to December 3, 2021. Some days, I did not have the energy, encouragement, or support to give. Some days, I didn't feel like talking. Some days, I didn't feel like being bothered. Some days, I didn't feel like pushing myself. Some days, I didn't feel like showing up. I recall the Brandi I was when I would check on people to see how they were doing, to offer words of support and encouragement. This Brandi was in a space where I was learning to be OK with not finding the strength to check in. It was OK to no longer pour from an empty cup, it was OK to not have the energy to entertain certain things, and it was OK to not be who I once was. It was OK to not be that person again.

When experiencing loss, you have to unlearn who you were to learn who you're becoming. I believe that loss reveals areas of your life that have been suppressed and dormant, and what needs to be healed and worked on.

Chapter 4

Finding New Purpose

What do you do now? Perhaps you were a loved one's caretaker, you spoke to your loved one on certain days of the week, or your loved one was your go-to person for everything, and now that they are gone, you find yourself lost, hopeless, and confused. The answer is to find a new purpose. Finding a new purpose in life is helping me to keep him alive. Finding a new purpose is giving me the strength to keep going. Finding a new purpose brings me joy when I'm able to help others who have experienced what I did.

On April 8, 2022, I posted on social media pictures of me that were taken at a speaking engagement I was a part of in March of that year. I shared, "I had the privilege and honor to be a guest speaker for The Cleansing, a two-day women's event. On Friday night, I encouraged women with steps they can take to become new. You might ask or even think, 'How am I able to do that when I'm grieving and learning what *new* means?' I tell you, it was GOD!

All I know is that my Boo posted on Facebook two years ago for my birthday, 'Keep doing what God has planned for you.' All I can do is that! Let God use me while He heals me simultaneously. You truly can do all things through Christ who strengthens you. This is what I mean when I say, 'Impacting lives one conversation at a time.'"

With those words in mind, "Keep doing what God planned for you," my heart was led to be a blessing to someone else, but in a more purposeful way. I believe God allowed me to be a caretaker for a short while to understand and experience all that it truly entails. It dropped in my spirit to raise funds for caregivers and for lung cancer in honor of my dad for my nonprofit's fundraiser in September. Being a caretaker takes a toll on your mind, body, and spirit, and it was now my duty to bless someone who was currently in my former shoes. I was able to raise enough funds to award four caretakers with life coaching, wellness service, and personal training sessions.

As I reflected over the year that was flying by, I couldn't help but have empathy every time someone I personally knew lost a parent or a close family member. I don't think it strange that God was using me to comfort them and provide words of encouragement. I believe God was using me to show them the God in me during their heartbreak, grief, and mourning.

God was even using me to help and support my line sister and business bestie during her time of becoming a caregiver for her father while she, too, watched her godfather fight cancer. I gave her advice and shared my experience when it came to filling out the paperwork for Medicare. It later amazed me how God used me to go through a situation such as this first to later go back and help those who were going through.

On August 17, 2022, I responded to my "little sister's" Instagram story that she had posted of her mom. I asked how she was doing, and she replied, "Not good, sis. We just found out that her tumor came back and is growing rapidly. We're bringing in hospice on Friday. There's nothing more they can do for her in terms of treatment. Everything rests in God's hands now." Immediately, I offered support and words of encouragement. I remember when the doctor told me he wished he could have been able to save my dad. I remember when we had to bring hospice in. I shared, "There's a scripture that says God comforts us so that we can comfort others. Trust me; since my dad passed, I know about five people who lost their father's and three people who lost their mothers! Honestly, as weird as it sounds, it helps my healing journey because I'm in the space. Trust me; someone who never lost a parent will never understand. Regardless, I will show up in the way God sees fit. It still boggles my mind that he's not here physically, but I promise I see signs of him every day."

She later shared, "Girl, I just had a thought for a future program that you can do. And I think that it can be devoted to people that have lost their parents and involve something around how they can honor their memory the same way you're doing the event in September in memory of your father. You can kind of spearhead it. You're creative and so innovative. But some type of program where people that have lost their parents, or maybe you can just devote it simply to children who have lost their parents because that is a different type of loss. But they can honor their loved one in some way. I just think that would be such a healing program, and girl, you would be the perfect person to lead it."

Chapter 5

Life After Death

Unfortunately, life is still moving on after the loss of a loved one while you are still grieving and mourning. There will come a point in time when you will have to live your life after death. It does not mean that you will forget them; it means that there's still life that God has purposed for you to live.

Following my father's celebration of life, I went to DC, as I had planned prior to his death, to see friends and attend a holiday party. I remember it was one of my first outings since my dad passed, and I took a picture and used the caption, "Life after death." Although I missed my Boo, I knew he would want me to still live my life.

Two weeks later, I made the decision to still attend my friend's 35th birthday party. She had asked me in March to pray for her on her 35th birthday after seeing a video of me praying for my friend at her 40th birthday earlier that year. She said that she totally understood if I decided to no longer do it, but I knew he would want me to continue living and doing what God called me to do. That would be the first time I prayed since the day my father passed. Who knew that because of my prayer over her, her cousin would ask me to pray and preach at her mother's funeral six months later.

Life after death looks like figuring out what that looks like. It's going to look different for everyone. After the heaviness of the first six months, I prayed and asked God for joy and to allow me to enjoy the summer. I desired to enjoy life, smile, be happy, and create new memories. God was faithful to grant my request. I traveled, enjoyed my summer nights, and found joy in life after death. I could hear my dad's voice saying, "What are you crying for? Live your life." I was international about having joy. I traveled, I danced, I laughed, I created new memories, and I was surrounded by love and light.

There is always life after death. It may not look like the life you had prior to the death of your loved one, but as long as we're still in the land of the living, God still has good things planned for us. There's healing, peace, love, and the presence of God.

Chapter 6

Honor Your Loved One

When a loved one is no longer here, honoring them is a way that helps you to not only cope, but find a way to help keep their spirit alive. I wanted to share with the world my new purpose and how I was going to honor my father after his death.

"In September 2021, Founder Brandi took on the responsibility of caretaker for her father, who was diagnosed with stage 4 lung cancer the day after Blessed by Brandi, Inc.'s Fall for the Possible Fundraising Brunch event. Unbeknownst to her, her father was determined to take the 14-hour train ride from South Carolina, where he resided and persevered in unbearable pain to support his Boo, as he affectionately called her. She would later find out it would be his last event.

Being in the hospital for a few weeks and contracting COVID-19, trying to regain his strength at the rehabilitation center, being unsuccessful in receiving approval for Medicaid in New Jersey, and now being considered uninsured were all key factors that played a part and delayed his ability to receive immediate treatment. Her father's oncologist empathized with his situation and informed her of the Amgen Safety Net Foundation. The foundation was going to cover all costs for treatment, but unfortunately, her father passed on December 3, 2021, a week before he received approval.

Brandi wants to be able to bless someone who has walked, or may walk, in the same shoes with wellness services after knowing firsthand the stress, frustration, and heaviness of being a caretaker. In honor of Brandi's father, her goal is to give back by helping other lung cancer patients have a successful survival story regardless of being uninsured."

On April 5, 2022, I posted on social media the day I launched my website for my nonprofit Blessed by Brandi, Inc. I posted, "To grieve and go back to work is one thing. But to grieve while trying to heal and trying to coach people with their life goals, provide spiritual support, and to encourage people through your faith-based business is another. I've found a new purpose since December 3, 2021. I stand here today, literally, with God's grace and strength. I honestly know it's only God who is pushing me because I don't know how, humanly speaking, I'm able to find words to encourage people and pray for people when I need to be encouraged and covered in prayer. With all that being said, I push through because at the end of the day, God is using me. There are people who are going through what I'm going through. So, in honor of my Boo, Blessed by Brandi, Inc. found a new purpose. My website has officially launched, and with mixed emotions, I find comfort in knowing there's a special purpose behind it. I'm raising funds for lung cancer patients and to provide holistic wellness services for three caretakers at my annual September event."

I was not looking forward to the month of June, as it marked the six-month anniversary of his death, Father's Day, and his birthday. Friends who lost their parents before me suggested and offered advice to find ways to honor him and to create new memories. With Father's Day and his birthday being a week apart, I wanted to keep the tradition going. I went to the store and purchased a Father's Day card. In that card, I poured my heart out like any other year, expressing my love and gratitude for him. For his birthday, I always send him an Outback Steakhouse gift card to treat him to dinner.

This year, my mother and grandmother accompanied me, and we went to Outback Steakhouse for lunch. I ordered his favorite meal: an 11-ounce Outback sirloin steak, medium rare, baked potato with butter, and a house salad. I ordered Crown Royal with ginger ale, which was the last drink he and I had together. I ordered a cheesecake to sing "Happy Birthday" to celebrate his life. Later, I popped a bottle of Moët Rosé champagne to toast to the years of having him in my life as my father. His birthday and Father's Day were not days to be sad; they were days to honor and celebrate the loving father that he was, the great memories we shared, the time we spent, his unconditional support, and the values he instilled in me.

When planning my September Cocktails and Kicks Fundraiser event, I wanted to do something extra special to honor my dad. This was the anniversary of the event he persevered to come to from SC. I know that he would be so proud of the work that I was doing, especially in honor of his name. I had an idea and partnered with my godsister, founder and candlemaker of the Honeyed Co., to give candles to my guests in honor of my Boo. She created two candles: one was in honor of him, and the second was reminiscent of the encounter I had with God the day he transitioned. The first candle is called Perseverance: "Rest if you must, but never give up" — BJEM. This was to honor the way he persevered in pain to get to New Jersey. I later found out that before he left SC he told his family and friends goodbye because he knew that would be the last time they saw him. The second candle is called Heaven on Earth: "Peace that surpasses all understanding is a piece from Heaven." I've never experienced a peace that surpasses all understanding. I could not comprehend how I witnessed my father take his last breath, close his eyes, and feel peace that surpassed what I was experiencing at the same time.

Chapter 7

Love Exists Beyond Space and Time

I'll never forget one of my dad's many visits and him expressing his unconditional love for me. He said, "I will always love you. I will love you until the last breath in my body." He was right. He was never a man who shied away from expressing how he felt. I didn't always tell him verbally when I was growing up, but as an adult, I expressed it in cards and on social media for his birthday and Father's Day. Periodically, I would go on his Facebook page and scroll through his wall to see what he posted. I came across all the birthday and Father's Day posts I tagged him in over the years.

June 21, 2015: "Happy Father's Day, Boo. Thank you for always being there, being a provider, and constantly showering me with your love. I appreciate the morals and values that you instilled in me, which have molded me into the woman I am today. Love ya, Boo!"

June 18, 2017: "Happy Father's Day to my Boo, John Barry McAlister Sr. You are truly a one-of-a-kind dad! The way you reminisce on every event in my life, or just moments where I made you proud, or how much you brag about me definitely doesn't go unnoticed. Thanks for always being there and reminding me that no man will ever love me more than you, hahahaha! Enjoy your day, Boo."

June 21, 2020: "Today, I woke up extra blessed, grateful, and thankful for you. As I reflect over every birthday, every church date, every Six Flags Great Adventures trip, every graduation, every Terpsy Dance show, my Cotillion, and now every *Heart to Heart* episode on IG, you are there, and have always been. To my Boo, Papa, Father (laughing emoji), wishing you an amazing Father's Day. I love you (kissy face)."

June 20, 2021: "The first relationship a girl has (or is supposed to have) is with her father. God blessed me with a special one, John McAlister! To my Boo: Happy Father's Day! Love you, and enjoy your day. Thank you for your unconditional love and support in all that I do (kissy emoji)."

December 4, 2021: "Hey, Boo, John McAlister! These past three months have truly been an emotional roller coaster. Who would've thought your story would end like this? It was a beautiful story that only God could have written. Over the past few years, the dynamic of our relationship changed. I went from being your daughter, to us arguing like husband and wife (laughing emoji) to becoming a mother figure by taking care of you. These are our last pictures I made sure to take with you, not knowing it would be so soon. You fought a good fight until the end. God answered my prayer to give you a new body, mind, and spirit, and to take the pain away. I am at peace knowing God heard and answered me. I love you, Boo; you know that! I'm truly going to miss you (insert crying face). It's still so surreal, but I'm glad I made you proud and gave you a reason to Bragg, LOL. See you later, Papa. Love, Boo."

December 5, 2021: "Boo, what can I say? I am you, and you are me. It wasn't until I got older that I started to see more of you in me. From being 'emotional' to being the life of the party, to celebrating every milestone in life, to being family oriented, and most importantly, spreading the word of God to other people. We argued, you got on every one of my last nerves (laughing emoji), you claim I got on yours, but let's be real (laughing emoji). Many people didn't have the opportunity to grow up with their father or even experience what a father's love is. I want to thank God today that I was able to experience that. You were far from perfect and made a lot of mistakes, BUT one thing you were perfect at was loving me with your all. You bragged about me and were my number-one fan. You never let me forget that you never wanted me. You didn't want a girl because of what you did back in your heyday (rolls eyes, LOL), and you didn't want a man to treat me in that manner. But once I was here, you realized that I was the best thing that ever happened to you (insert purple heart). You drilled in me that no man will ever love me like you do, but I realized he's not supposed to. His love will be a different kind of love that can never be compared to yours. I'm going to be fine! I was blessed with you for 37 years, and God made sure it was me and you ,until the very end. I know you're gonna watch over me. You're probably trying to tell God right now which blessing to send me and God is probably telling you to chill; he got this (laughing emoji). I love you, Boo! You have instilled and equipped me with everything I need to live my life. In your last days, God prepared me for my next chapter! I know you're going to be soooo proud. I'll see you later (kissy face)."

December 3, 2022: "December 3, 2021; I remember it like it was yesterday. I watched you fight the pain and tell the Lord you were coming. I laid on your chest and watched you take your last breath. I don't know if I'm numb, in disbelief, or perhaps in denial that you have not been here for a whole year. My mind still can't fully fathom that in 365 days, I haven't heard your voice, you haven't called me, I haven't picked you up from Newark Penn Station, we haven't talked about God, you haven't called me Boo, and you haven't told me, 'Daddy loves you.' Although you haven't done those things, you did show up in other ways this year. That has given me peace that surpasses all understanding and has comforted me. It honestly feels like a long week that's going to last forever. I think about you every single day, I talk about you any chance I get, and I look forward to seeing signs of your presence showing up. Your presence is what I use to keep your spirit alive. It's hard to believe that you are not physically here because I still see you. I love you more than I've ever told you, and I miss you more than words can express. Thank you for OVER-loving me for 37 years. I didn't understand it then, but I do now. A father's love is something special (heart). I felt your love more this year than I did my entire life. Your love, God's love, and the love from others is what kept me from feeling the pain of a broken heart. I love you, Boo! My number-one guy! (kissy face)"

Chapter 8

Time Heals

Contrary to popular belief, most people don't agree with the statement, "Time heals." I would like to challenge you to think about that statement from another perspective. Most of the time when we hear that statement, we are in the middle of the agony, unable to see past the pain, unable to function, and heartbroken beyond belief. The thought of time healing seems impossible. But let's put it into a different context. Think about a time you may have fallen and bruised your knee, pulled a muscle and the pain was so sharp, or even experienced the pain from a hangnail or paper cut. Depending on the person, it takes time for the bruise to heal, for the pain to subside, or for the wound to close. Can you recall over time how the pain from those physical experiences is no longer there?

Or have you ever had to heal from a breakup? Job loss? I thought about the times when I was heartbroken from breakups, disappointed from not getting a call back from the jobs I interviewed for, crushed from being laid off twice in my career, distraught from not seeing the manifestation of my heart's desires, or angry with God for not answering my prayers when I wanted Him to. I think about how it took time for me to heal from those experiences. I think about how it took time for my faith to come back stronger. I think about the time it took to heal my broken heart. I think about the time it took to heal to the point where the sting from the memories became a thing of the past. I think about how I'm no longer broken in those areas. I think about how it truly did take time to heal.

When it comes to healing, you cannot rush your process. The amount of time it takes to heal is different for everyone. As I reflect on my healing process from the loss of my father, I recall how I used to count every Friday that he was gone. I stopped counting on Friday, June 3, 2022 when it hit 26 weeks, or six months. I recall that every Friday for four-and-a-half months, I wore the same outfit that I wore the day my father passed. I think about how I used to get anxious every Friday between the hours of 12 p.m. and 4 p.m. because those were the hours during which he transitioned. I think about the Fridays when I would sit in the area where he passed and have a gut-wrenching cry. I think about the times when a deep and heavy sadness would fall upon me.

When I reached the one-year anniversary of his death, I reflected on how things became lighter, ceased, and stopped. It took time.

"Time heals" doesn't mean that you won't miss them.

"Time heals" doesn't mean you won't be sad.

"Time heals" doesn't mean you won't relive the moment they left.

"Time heals" doesn't mean that you will forget about them.

"Time heals" doesn't mean that you won't have your moments.

"Time heals" simply means that over time, God will mend your broken heart. To mend means to repair (something that is broken or damaged), return to health, heal, or improve an unpleasant situation, especially a disagreement. It means that God will lighten the heaviness and weight of your loss. It means God will reduce the sting of the pain. It means God will take the pain away.

Most people say time doesn't heal because they are still stuck in the time the loved one passed, stuck in time of when the pain first hit because time is passing by while the pain and memories have remained. When death comes suddenly or unexpectedly, we may experience the stages of grief that are beyond our ability to control or even comprehend. Depending on the circumstance of your loved one's transition, the stage of acceptance may be the hardest and take the longest to move through. No one wants to accept that their loved one is no longer here physically. But what I've experienced through acceptance is that healing can begin to take place. It's not going to happen overnight because it takes time. Allow God to heal your broken spirit, bandage your wounds, and mend your broken heart.

Don't get stuck in the pain; don't get stuck in the depression; don't get stuck in the agony; don't get stuck in the guilt; don't get stuck in the trauma. You have the power to choose to feel all the feels, but not get stuck. You have the power to choose to allow time to heal.

I spent years envisioning the pain I would feel the day the inevitable would happen.

Kirk Franklin has a song titled, "He'll Take the Pain Away." The lyrics are:

He'll take the pain away, I know.

Though you been searching

For such a long time,

Searching for hope

And some peace of mind,

There's a friend

Who will step in on time.

He'll take the pain away, I know.

You've been searching here and all of there, and all God can take the pain away.

I tried him for myself, and ooooooh, I'm a living witness that God can take the pain away.

He'll take the pain away.

Hold on; don't give up.

If any man be in Jesus, He'll take the pain away.

If any man be in Jesus brand new, He'll take the pain away."

My dad resided in St. Helena, SC since 2005, and my biggest fear had always been that I'd get a phone call from a relative or his friend saying that someone found him no longer alive and that I would have to go to SC to identify him and send his body back to New Jersey.

I had always mentally prepared myself for his story to end that way, BUT GOD! I imagined the pain, agony, and anguish I'd be in on the day I would get "the call," BUT GOD!

God had a beautiful ending of my father's story that took my pain away. Since my father's wishes were to be cremated, my brother and I decided we would go to SC to spread his ashes. Fear, anxiety, and worry began to infiltrate my mind, body, and spirit at the thought of envisioning how reality would play out. I had thoughts of entering into his trailer and rummaging through his belongings, and fear tried to paralyze me, BUT GOD!

My brother decided to go down in January ahead of me, and then we would go together in March for the three-month anniversary. My brother went through my father's belongings and made the decision to have his trailer removed from the property so that I wouldn't have to deal with another traumatic experience in March.

When we arrived in March, a relative informed me that my father's trailer was removed. When I picked my brother up from the airport, he was surprised at how quickly it had been removed. He and I went to the property to see for ourselves, and, in fact, it was gone.

In that moment, I realized and understood that God took the pain away and saved me from another heartache. Once again, God took the pain away. God worked all things together for my good on what I expected to be a painful trip because I love Him and am called according to His purpose. God planned for it to be the most beautiful experience ever. I met relatives and some of my dad's friends, who shared stories that were consistent with who he was. They shared how much he was missed. This brought me comfort, peace, and joy, and made my heart smile again.

Chapter 9

Weeping May Endure for a Night, But Joy Comes in the Morning

Grief and mourning is an emotional rollercoaster. It's a wave of emotions, and you never know what will trigger the pain or what will bring a smile to your face. No matter what, weeping may endure for the night, but joy comes in the morning. I remember that for the first six months, I would cry as soon as I began to speak about my dad, and then, moments later, a sense of peace would come over me.

The day before my 38th birthday, I remember having joy, laughing on FaceTime with my friends, and getting excited about my upcoming solo trip. It wasn't until the night came and I began listening to the playlist that I created for him. I came across my first birthday picture of me and him, and then I came across the last birthday picture he and I took together. A deep sadness came over me as I began to reflect on how I spent my birthday last year by visiting him in the rehabilitation center.

I will never forget the encounter I had with him that day. When I arrived that morning, he was sleeping, and then he looked over at me. He asked me what my plans were for the day, and I shared with him that I was going to the spa and then dinner. Next, he asked, "How's your big-headed uncle doing?" I was caught off guard, and I asked, "What uncle?" He responded, "Robert." My heart stopped, and I froze. His brother Robert had died three years prior, and I did not know what to say. My heart was saying one thing, and my mind was saying another. I couldn't find nor utter the words to remind him that he had passed three years ago. I responded, "He's fine," and he said, "OK," grabbed his head, and went back to sleep. Never in my 37 years of life has he forgot to tell me happy birthday or ask me about a relative who was deceased. Later that afternoon, I checked Facebook, and with tears of joy and sadness, I read what would be his last happy birthday wish to me. He messaged me, "Happy birthday, lady. Enjoy your day. Love Always, Your Boo, Daddy."

After reminiscing and weeping that night, the next morning, there was joy. It was my birthday, and I was excited to go on my solo birthday trip to Arizona. As I traveled, I felt love, peace, joy, and my father's presence with me the entire trip. The first birthday without him physically here, I believe he made sure that it was filled with joy.

Chapter 10

Navigating Through Your New Reality

The hardest part about grieving the death of a loved one, a dream deferred, or plans not panning out the way you envisioned is accepting a new life that changed unexpectedly, suddenly, without notice, and in a way you were never prepared for. We are then left with learning how to cope and navigate through our new reality.

I would say that when navigating through your new reality, you will experience similar stages in the grieving process. When death comes suddenly or unexpectedly, we may experience stages of grief that are beyond our ability to control or even comprehend. Depending on the circumstances of your loved one's transition, the stage of acceptance may be the hardest and take the longest to move through.

No one wants to accept that their loved one is no longer here physically. What I experienced through acceptance is that healing can begin to take place. With acceptance, your heart will open, and you will learn how to navigate through your new reality and take steps toward your new life.

In March of 2021, I didn't realize that I was at the beginning of navigating through a new reality. After moving back home, contracting COVID, experiencing the end of my unemployment, not receiving the part-time job position, finding out my dad had stage 4 lung cancer, and becoming his caregiver, I was spiritually and emotionally depleted. I was hit with a new reality in every area of my life. All I remember was going through the motions. My new life was not what I planned, dreamed, or envisioned, and the majority of my life's changes came without warning.

On December 21, 2022, I had a coaching session with my business and life coach, and he asked, "What does getting back on track look like?" As I reflected on that question, it really meant, "What does navigating through your new reality look like?" I had to take time to think about it because I had never experienced a loss in every area of my life in the same year before. I responded:

- » Disconnecting from the world when I need alone time
- » Being still
- » Not pushing through when I don't have the strength to
- » Taking much-needed time for myself
- » Feeling all the feels of the grieving process
- » Not rushing the process
- » Not compartmentalizing my feelings

I took the time to implement these steps into my navigation. I was a new person, and I had to not only navigate through a new reality, but also navigate through emotions I'd never felt and had suppressed over the years. I had to navigate understanding that I would never be the same person I was and having to get comfortable with this version of myself whom I didn't know. I had to navigate by showing myself grace and being OK with not showing up for people how I once did.

I learned that on this journey, it's an emotional roller coaster of highs and lows, good days and bad days, and crying and laughing. The navigation is not a linear one; it's filled with twists and turns and accepting that you have to take it minute by minute, hour by hour, and day by day. There's no right or wrong way to navigate this road. It will look different for everyone, and that's OK. The keys to the journey are to accept that your new life will look different than the one you had the day before the loss, and to allow God to be the guide on this road.

Navigating through your new reality is learning to live without your loved one, making adjustments, perhaps keeping yourself busy, and becoming acclimated without them in your life.

Chapter 11

Never Would Have Made It

I made it through year one of life without the physical presence of my dad on earth. I made it to the first anniversary with love, comforting words, and prayers from others. The day was not as heavy as I anticipated it to be. The amount of people who loved on me and thought enough about me to reach out to check on me or to tell me they were praying for me was unbelievable. The power of love is real. I never would have made it, had it not been for God, my angel, and the people God sent to comfort me.

The next day, I woke up with joy and was so moved by the experience that I wanted to share the good news with the world. I shared on social media a video I captured of a sun peeking through the clouds hours before it was the anniversary of my father's time of death on the day of his one-year death anniversary. It had rained all day, and then, around 3:15 p.m., the sun came out. At that moment, I knew it was my dad peeking through to let me know he's fine, he's at peace, and he has been with me everyday.

I shared, "God is more than good. I'm still in awe of His miracles, signs, wonders, peace, and love. Thank you to everyone who loved on me yesterday, texted, called, sent prayers, and shared comforting words. God is real, and prayers work. And Boo showed up after crying tears of joy (raining) all morning. I was able to capture Heaven on earth. I promise you, this year, I experienced and encountered God in a new way. When God says He will give you peace that surpasses all understanding, believe Him. When God says you can do all things through Christ who strengthens you, believe Him and take Him at His word. I encourage everyone to spend more time with God in His word and apply it to your life. To those who are still grieving and mourning, I want to let you know to lean on God more than ever. He will carry you through and heal your broken heart and spirit. Spreading and sending God's love, light, peace, and blessings."

I never would've made it without God. I know it to be true because I know God for myself. After watching Boo take his last breath, I laid on his chest, closed his eyes, kissed his forehead, and put my Pray the Impossible mask on him. A sense of peace came over me as I looked at him resting in peace. It was a peace I had never experienced before. It was a peace that surpassed understanding and the out-of-body experience I was having. I had always imagined that the day my father transitioned, I would be rolling on the floor, brokenhearted; but instead, God carried me through it and gave me His peace and His strength to witness his five-hour transition.

I never would've made it from December 3, 2021 to December 3, 2022 without God, my family and friends, and those who God sent on my path.

In the words of Marvin Sapp:

Never would have made it
Never could have made it without You
I would have lost it all
But now I see how You were there for me

I'm stronger, I'm wiser
I'm better, much better

When I look back
Over all You brought me through
I can see that You were the One
I held on to

Through my storm and my test
Because You were there
To carry me through my mess

Chapter 12

The Author of Our Lives

God is the author and finisher of our lives. He knows the end from the beginning. In this life on earth, only two things are predetermined: our birth date and the date of our death. The dash in between is filled with blessings, lessons, trials, and triumphs. I reflected on the amount of people I know who lost a loved one after my loss, the circumstances surrounding how their loved ones passed, and how everyone handles their grief and mourning processes differently. It inspired me to post, "Wisdom Wednesdays: We were never promised a life that we planned; we're promised a life that God has planned for us."

When death occurs, it's never a part of the plans we make or envision for our lives. Although we know death is inevitable, it's not an event that we include in our life plans. We could and would never think to plan the age we will be when we lose a loved one, how the loved one will leave this earth, or even the pain we will feel when the loved one is no longer physically here. We also forget that the beginning and ending of our life stories were already written before we were formed. God already knew when and how our last day on this earth would end. When death occurs suddenly or happens tragically, or when one is suffering until the end, it's not a surprise to God. Humanly speaking, we cannot understand, accept, or believe that God would allow it to happen in such a way. I believe that's what makes the grieving process hard because we are left in a state of shock, angered, in denial, depressed, and unable to accept that life will never be the same without our loved one.

These thoughts led me to think about God's plan. Think about Jesus for a minute. God sent Jesus into this world to die for our sins so that we can be in relationship with Him. Jesus was 33 years old, and while on earth, he wept, was angry, grieved, and experienced excruciating pain. He was beaten, stripped of his garments, forced to carry his cross that he was later nailed to, and then crucified. In his agony, he cried out to God. He said in Luke 22:42, "Father, if You are willing, please take this cup of suffering away from me; yet, I want Your will to be done, not mine." God chose to not take the pain away because His plan needed to be fulfilled. Jesus had to fulfill the purpose so that we can be made right with God through His sacrifice.

You, too, may be experiencing pain that is unbearable, you may not be able to comprehend why your loved one's life was cut short, or you may not be able to fathom the trauma around how your loved one was taken from you, but God is the author and finisher of our lives and knows the plans He has for us. 2 Corinthians 12:8–10 states, "Three different times, I begged the Lord to take it away.

Each time, He said, 'My grace is all you need. My power works best in weakness.' So, now, I am glad to boast about my weaknesses, so that the power of Christ can walk through me. That's why I take pleasure in my weaknesses, and in the insults, hardships, persecutions, and troubles that I suffer for Christ. For when I am weak, then I am strong."

God's ultimate plan is to draw us closer to Him by any means necessary. Sometimes, the purpose of the plan includes pain, but in the end, we know that God works all things together for the good of those who love Him and are called according to His purpose. If Jesus, the son of God, experienced pain, who are we to be exempt from pain? For God knows the plans He has for us, and those plans may include the untimely (in our minds) and unexpected death of a loved one. God could be using this as an opportunity to draw closer to Him, to reveal Himself to you, to experience Him as your Heavenly Father, to teach you to fully depend on Him, and to give you a new purpose amongst the land of the living.

Chapter 13

My Greatest Loss Turned Into a Purposeful WIN

March 31, 2022

Dear Brandi from 2021,

Girl! You have gone through a lot! You endured a lot! You also experienced major losses this year that you never intended! But truly, the grace of God has kept you. I remember you said you wanted to encounter God in a new way. It's not until a full year later that you received revelation and insight! Let's talk about what you lost.

In January, you decided to move back home due to your upcoming financial situation. You made that move on 3/31/21. You contracted COVID in July and lost your sense of smell. Later that summer, you and your last paying client for coaching with Pray the Impossible ended her coaching agreement. In September, you did not get the part-time job position that originally presented itself as promising. Within that same week, unemployment ended, and you found out Boo was diagnosed with stage 4 lung cancer. Your faith was tested, and you lost your faith in the fire. You lost a part of yourself. You lost your praise and worship. You lost your personal spiritual alignment. You lost your Boo! Through it all, you're still here! You are still standing! Today, you smile and rejoice because you have changed your perspective. Greater is truly on the way. The enemy thought he could take you out, but God said, "Not her."

Today, you heard God's voice say, "There's a shift!" Things have definitely shifted in your mind, heart, and spirit. Today marks the end of this season of loss! You are stronger, wiser, and more equipped to receive all that God has for you. You've got your fire back, and nothing can stop you now. Focus on God! He's going to add everything you've been praying and believing in Him for. Remove the doubt! You know what God is able to do! You've seen God do the impossible! He's been testing your faith because of His glory that is associated with your blessing. Remember, God is able! He can, and He will! Keep your eyes on Him. Be intentional, and don't allow what you can't see to stop you from seeing! Not everyone can handle with grace all that you have. God chose you for this!

You learned to trust God like never before. You experienced His perfect peace that surpasses all understanding. God truly provided and made a way for you! It's you and God! You've trusted in Him in the small things, so now, He can trust you with the big things. I'm excited to see the blessings that are coming your way. I'm more excited for you to receive your heart's desires and answered prayers.

Love Always,

2022 Brandi

The loss of my personal space (apartment), having health challenges, being unable to find employment, experiencing financial difficulties, and losing my father in the same year were great losses. But the purposeful win in the great losses was experiencing God. The purposeful win was encountering God. The purposeful win was witnessing Heaven on earth. The purposeful win was knowing that God is faithful and God's word is true, and learning God in a new way. The purposeful win was knowing firsthand that a great loss can turn into a purposeful win because God causes all things together for the good of those who love Him and who are called according to His purpose.

The below scriptures helped me to recognize that although I experienced a great loss, God turned it into a purposeful win:

Matthew 5:4 — "God blesses those who mourn, for they will be comforted."

As I mourned, God blessed me in ways I could never think were possible. God sent people my way to pour their love, prayers, and comforting words into my life. I used this as fuel to keep going, to keep living, and to see God's blessings upon my life.

Do you believe that God will bless you as you mourn? Have you experienced blessings in the form of comfort?

____

____

____

____

____

____

____

____

____

____

1 Thessalonians 4:13 — "And now, dear brothers and sisters, we want you to know what will happen to the believers who have died so you will not grieve like people who have no hope."

I understood and experienced grieving with hope and witnessed the difference of grieving without hope. I knew my father went to be with the Lord as he called out to Him in his last hours. I experienced and saw God's hand at work the day He transitioned. I saw how God still used me to share words of hope and inspiration on Pray the Impossible and Blessed by Brandi. I had enough hope to believe that I would see signs of my father show up every day for me through different signs. I still knew God was good through it all. I knew my father was my angel and was making a way for me, protecting me, and working with God to orchestrate personal blessings.

Is your grieving process one with hope or without hope? Is it hard to hope that it will get better over time?

____

____

____

____

____

____

____

____

____

____

2 Corinthians 1:4 — "He comforts us in all our troubles so that we can comfort others. When they are troubled, we will be able to give them the same comfort God has given us."

God blew my mind. I would have never thought how therapeutic it is to comfort others during your time of need. Comforting others and sharing my story was a part of my healing process. I know two handfuls of people who lost parents and a handful who lost a loved one. I could not help but to send encouraging words. To share with them my coping mechanisms. To give them the comfort that was poured into my life. I understood that my purpose in this new season of my life was for me to go back and be an example of God's strength. From speaking at my friend's aunt's funeral to pouring into a friend whose father passed on the one-year anniversary of my dad's death, I knew I had no choice but to be a vessel of God.

Do you have trouble comforting others when you are grieving? In what ways can you be a blessing to someone who may go through a similar experience?

____

____

____

____

____

____

____

____

____

____

____

Psalms 68:5 — "Father to the fatherless, defender of widows—this is God, whose dwelling is holy."

I understood that my relationship with God had changed. I was no longer coming to God as His faithful servant. I was now fatherless and needed a father. I had to learn to approach God as my Heavenly father. I had to change my perspective, as my needs had changed. I now approached the throne of God as His daughter. I had to work on forming a relationship with God from a child's perspective. I needed His arms to wrap around; I needed God to carry me; I needed God to mend my heart and spirit; I needed to be comforted; I needed to be reassured that I was going to be OK; I needed to learn to depend on God.

How are you approaching God during this time? Are you allowing yourself to become a child again? Are you expecting God to care for you like a parent?

____

Galatians 6:2 — "Carry one another's burdens, and in this way you will fulfill the law of Christ."

In this season of life, God knew who I needed and what I needed. My sorority sister and I formed a deeper and stronger bond. She lost her mother five weeks after I lost my father. We checked on each other often, especially on significant days like Mother's Day and Father's Day, on our parents' birthdays, and on their death anniversaries. Whenever I needed to vent or cry, I called her, and vice versa. We shared each other's burdens, sharing our feelings, unloading the burden of the weight of the situations that were happening in our families that were affecting us. Through it all, one was strong when the other was weak, one was comforting while the other was being comforted, and one carried the burden when the other could no longer carry it.

How can you carry the burden of someone who is grieving?

____

____

____

____

____

____

____

____

____

____

____

____

Philippians 4:7 — "Then you will experience God's peace, which exceeds anything we can understand."

I think this might be my new favorite scripture. God is, was, and will forever be faithful to His word. I've had peace in situations and peace in the middle of storms, but I had finally experienced peace that surpassed all understanding. I can't even begin to describe or articulate this peace. I still can't believe the moments I shared with my dad in his final hours on earth. God already knew how the story was going to end, and peace was what He gave me. There will be things in life we will never understand or comprehend, but God gave me His peace to trust in Him through it all. God gave me His peace to get through the situation because there was purpose in it. God gave me His peace to trust that this is not the end, but a new beginning was on the horizon.

Are you ready to receive peace that surpasses all understanding? Are you ready to rest in God and let Him reveal to you the purpose in this?

____

____

____

____

____

____

____

____

____

____

____

____

____

James 4:8 — "Come close to God, and God will come close to you."

I had not felt close to God since March 2021. Although I was thriving as a Spiritual Friendvisor with Pray the Impossible, my personal relationship with Him felt like it had flatlined. In April of 2022, I read a book called *The Circle*, and it brought me closer to God. I started to find a piece of myself that had left over a year ago. In October, on my solo birthday trip, I set my intentions to get back into alignment spiritually. I began journaling again. I recognized that when I journal, I feel closest to God, and God speaks and reveals things to me while I'm writing.

What can you do to draw closer to God?

____

____

____

____

____

____

____

____

____

____

____

Ecclesiastes 3:4 — "A time to cry, and a time to laugh. A time to grieve, and a time to dance."

Counting the Fridays, counting the months, wearing the same outfit—at some point, God said it was time to laugh and dance again. For the first six months, I cried frequently at the thought of missing him or whenever I spoke about him. I felt a deep sadness, listened to the playlist every morning that reminded me of him, and stared at his pictures in disbelief. But I prayed and asked God to experience joy for the summer. I wanted to dance, laugh, and enjoy life again, and God changed the times and seasons. What a difference a year makes. December 2021 and January 2022 were heavy and dark. In December 2022 and January 2023, God said the load is light, He will carry the burden, and it's time for me to experience the fullness of joy that He had set aside for me for an appointed time.

Are you ready to dance, laugh, and smile again? How are you working through your season and time of grief?

____

____

____

____

____

____

____

____

____

____

____

____

____

Lamentations 3:20 — "I will never forget this awful time, as I grieve over my loss."

I will never forget December 3, 2021. I reminded myself every Friday and every month. Anytime I spoke with someone and a situation reminded me of my loss, I shared my experience. It was my way of keeping him alive. But over time, God began to mend my heart and gave me unspeakable joy that trumped the promptings to count the weeks. Although the one-year anniversary of his death has passed, it is a memory that will live with me for the rest of my life. Time has proven that grief does get lighter, but I will always have moments where the memory brings tears to my eyes and my heart.

What can you do to bring honor to your loved one's name by keeping their memory alive?

____
____
____
____
____
____
____
____
____
____
____
____
____
____
____
____
____

2 Corinthians 2:4 — "I wrote that letter in great anguish with a troubled heart and many tears. I didn't want to grieve you, but I wanted to let you know how much love I have for you."

Thank God for social media. That was my outlet. Anytime I missed my Boo, I went to social media to post a video or picture, and I poured my heart out. I would often write him messages on his Facebook wall to let him know how much I missed him and how much he is missed.

Would you be open to writing a letter or message to your loved one expressing your love for them? What are some practical tools or techniques you can implement to communicate your love to them?

____

____

____

____

____

____

____

____

____

____

____

____

Psalms 34:18 — "The Lord is close to the brokenhearted, and he rescues those whose spirits are crushed."

God must have been close to me. There is no way, humanly speaking, that I was able to grieve, encourage and inspire people through Pray the Impossible and Blessed by Brandi, Inc., and comfort those who were also grieving. I remember the days when I cried. I remember reading devotionals about grieving; I remember following social media groups and pages about grieving. Those outlets helped to mend my heart. The more I spoke and shared my story, whether in person or posting on social media, I felt a sense of comfort come over me after I poured out my feelings. My spirit no longer felt crushed.

Do you feel the presence of God in your moments of grief and mourning? How do you feel after you let out a cry?

____
____
____
____
____
____
____
____
____
____
____
____

Matthew 11:30 — "For my yoke is easy to bear, and the burden I give you is light."

December 3, 2021 and January 2022 were heavy. Experiencing my first Father's Day, his first birthday, and my first birthday without my dad was heavy. Learning to grieve while carrying my brother's grief was heavy. Being anxious, feeling triggered every time I heard of someone I know who lost a loved one, and trying to learn who I've become and was becoming was heavy. God knew the burden, the weight, I was carrying was heavy. He blessed me on December 3, 2022 with His yoke and burden. The one-year anniversary was light. The month of December was light. January 2023 was light. God took on the weight of my burdens and gave me a burden that was light.

What is keeping you from giving God the weight of your burden? Do you believe that God wants to take on your pain and burden?

____

____

____

____

____

____

____

____

____

____

____

____

____

____

Psalms 30:11 — "You have turned my mourning into joyful dancing. You have taken away my clothes of mourning and clothed me with joy."

With God giving me His yoke, which is light, the one-year anniversary ushered in a shift. Waking up with joy the day after set the tone for the ending and beginning of the year. I no longer looked for signs for him to show up, I had unspeakable joy, and I basked in the love I felt during the holidays. As I entered the new year, I felt different, and it felt different. It felt as if my mourning clothes were gone, and I was now clothed with joy. The new clothes felt and looked good.

When did you take off your mourning clothes? How did it feel to be clothed with joy?

Chapter 14

How to Turn a Great Loss into a Purposeful Win

Grief is no respecter of person. Loss is no respecter of person. As long as we are living, we are all going to experience loss at some point in our lifetimes. Whether it's the loss of a loved one, job, relationship, home, or finances, grief will always be associated with it, but it doesn't have to end there. We can turn loss into a purposeful win when we understand that even in death, loss, or heartbreak, it can be used for a greater good that is bigger than us.

Turning a great loss into a purposeful win is no easy feat, but with hard work, intentionality, transparency, and openness, it can be achievable. Remember, the work starts within. The work begins with you.

You may be asking yourself, *What's next? What am I supposed to do? Where do I begin? How do I start?*

Step 1: Don't Skip Your Grieving and Mourning Process

Grief: deep sorrow, especially that caused by someone's death.

Mourning: the expression of deep sorrow for someone who has died.

This first step is ALWAYS going to look different for everyone. It may look like crying every day, it may look like keeping yourself busy, it may look like visiting a loved one at the cemetery every week, it may look like speaking about the loss to anyone who would listen, it may look like a state of depression, it may look like being angry and questioning God, and it may even look like your life is spiraling out of control. There is no road map or right way to grieve and mourn. The grieving and mourning process brings up emotions you suppressed over the years, it brings up emotions you never experienced, it brings up unhealed trauma, and it brings up memories—sometimes painful ones—from situations that were left unaddressed and unresolved. No matter what it looks like or feels like, it's imperative that you not only go through it, but grow through it.

This step is the most important one. Without this step, you will not be able to fully begin your healing journey, operate from a space of openness, or begin to navigate through your new reality. In this step, there are coping mechanisms, experiences, skills, techniques, and tools that will aid in your journey.

Take as much time as you need — Please do not allow anyone to tell you how long you should grieve or mourn your loss. Most people do not understand that with loss, other emotions and feelings resurface simultaneously. It's critical to take your time to work through each emotion that you are feeling. It's OK to feel everything. Running from the pain, heartache, or sorrow will only delay this step and your healing. God needs time to work through the complexities and intricate parts of your hurt, trauma, and heartache.

Grief Counseling/Therapy — There may be emotions that are too big to handle and too complicated to understand. Receiving professional help is OK. There are issues that have been buried and emotions that are resurfacing, and having someone walk you through it will only benefit you. It will provide the support you need from a community of people or an individual that friends and family cannot offer you.

Acknowledge and Honor Your Emotions — Anytime we are hurt, we tend to put up a defense mechanism to numb ourselves and refrain from feeling pain, sadness, or even weakness. Acknowledging and honoring your feelings makes you human. We have to normalize sitting in our feelings, but not becoming stuck there. Acknowledging and honoring our feelings will help us to face and get to the root of the issue that has caused us emotional damage, harm, and heartbreak. This will allow us to cleanse ourselves of old toxic feelings and allow healthy ones to enter into our life.

What does your grieving process look like? What steps can you take to work through your grief?

Step 2: Show Yourself Grace

You are doing the best that you can due to the circumstances. We may question ourselves or even consider thoughts of *should have, would have, could have* to explain why this happened. Forgive yourself of guilt, and forgive yourself for what you were not able to control. You don't have to rush your healing, grieving, or mourning process. This is a delicate situation, and you have to be handled with care and love.

We try to go back to who we were before the loss, but we have to realize we will never be that person again. With loss comes a new beginning, a new reality, and a new you. Show yourself grace as you learn, unlearn, and relearn who you were before the loss, who you became since the loss, and who you're becoming after the loss. It's OK to take time for yourself to get comfortable with being uncomfortable in this unfamiliar territory of healing, being restored, and becoming new. Show yourself grace by giving yourself permission to spend time alone in your thoughts, not show up for everyone else, and set boundaries. Grace is being kinder to yourself, creating a self-care routine, and not forcing your former self to reappear. Give yourself permission to work through your emotions.

What can you do to show yourself grace? What self-care routine can you implement?

Step 3: Lean On God

Whether you say God, Creator, Almighty, or Source in regards to the higher power you believe in, this step is what will carry you through the rest of your days. This step will carry you through your challenging days. This step will carry you through your sad days. This step will carry you through your lonely days. This step will carry you through your good days. God uses situations like the death of a loved one to draw us closer to Him. God wants us to depend on Him for healing, restoration, and the mending of our broken spirits.

There will be days where you don't know how you're going to make it through, can't find the strength to go on, or can't see how you can live life without that person. I'm here to tell you to lean on God. God is our source, creator, the most high, and all things we will ever need Him to be. In our weakness, God will give us his strength to get up, to live, and to find new meaning in life. God wants us to cry out to Him so that He can go into the secret place to give us what we need to become whole again.

Leaning on God allows Him to reveal His character to you and show you how much He cares about you. Leaning on God will give you clarity and a new perspective from His point of view. Leaning on God will give you hope. Leaning on God will give you faith. Leaning on God will give you comfort. Leaning on God will give you peace that surpasses all understanding. Leaning on God will bring your smile back. Leaning on God will give you joy. Leaning on God will give you hope. Leaning on God will give you a new purpose.

In what ways can you begin to lean on God? How can you depend on your spirituality and less on yourself to welcome healing and comfort?

Step 4: Create New Memories

The first year of loss can be the hardest, but creating new memories can help to ease the rawness of it. If it's a first birthday, first holiday, or first milestone without your loved one, creating new memories will help to honor them and keep their memory alive. If it's their first birthday, perhaps celebrate their birthday at their favorite restaurant. If it's the first Mother's Day or Father's Day, purchase a card and write a note in the card as if they were still here. If it's your wedding day or baby shower, create an "In Loving Memory" table with pictures or memorabilia of them. If it's the one-year anniversary of their transition, host a memorial or release balloons in their memory. It's all about creating new memories to express your love for your loved one. Whether it was five years or 55 years that you were given to experience them, it's about creating memories that will turn your mourning into joy.

What are some creative ways you can create new memories? How can you honor your loved one?

Step 5: Turn the Pain into Purpose with Power

Perhaps your loved one was ill, perhaps your loved one passed suddenly, or perhaps your loved one's transition was tragic—no matter how it happened, pain is what we are left with. One thing I know about God is that He will use our pain for His purpose. God will not let the pain we experience be in vain. There's unleashed power residing within us that comes from pain. We just have to tap into it.

There are people who lost a loved one before you, and there are people who will lose a loved one after you; the question becomes, *How can you turn your pain into purpose?* The answer is using your loss, pain, and experience to help someone else. There's something powerful about sharing your story to encourage others. There's something powerful about comforting others through your healing journey. There's something powerful about being a blessing to someone in need. There's something powerful about letting God use you in your brokenness the way He sees fit. There's something powerful about sharing your experience to help someone who is currently going through what you endured.

The purpose God gives you may be to bring awareness to an illness your loved one battled with. The purpose God gives you may be for you to be the example of what grieving with God looks like. The purpose God gives you may be to write a book to shed light on your experience with loss. The purpose God gives you may be to form a foundation in honor of your loved one. The purpose God gives you may be to turn your life around. The purpose God gives you may be to reconcile relationships with people who God ordained to be in your life. God will give you His power to go forth in purpose in the midst of pain.

What is the pain teaching you? How can you use this pain to help someone else?

These are steps that are meant to be repeated. This is a journey, and there will be moments when you feel as if you're losing, but working through these steps will help you to have a purposeful win. The purposeful win is about you. Winning in healing. Winning in overcoming what was sent to destroy you. Winning in having a relationship with God. Winning in managing and feeling your emotions. Winning in seeking professional and wise counsel to be a better you. Winning in thriving after a loss. Winning in turning your pain into purpose. Winning in navigating your new reality. Winning in being restored. Winning in knowing it's going to get better. Winning at fighting and never giving up. Winning at showing up for yourself. Winning at finding hope and light in the darkness. Winning at getting your joy back.

Chapter 15

Addressing Your Loss So That You Can Purposefully WIN

You may feel alone in what you're currently experiencing, but there is a community of people who, like you, are experiencing loss, struggling to accept their new reality, and unable to turn their pain into purpose.

The hardest part about it all is trying to navigate through a new life that you did not plan, expect, or prepare for.

I, too, have had my share of impossible situations and life-changing moments that I've had to navigate through.

I may not have always had the answers, understood why, or comprehended what God was doing, but as I look back, I see and know it was bigger than me. It was all for a purpose. Everything I lost; I gained a purposeful win.

As a Spiritual Friendvisor, a friend who gives advice based on godly wisdom, Certified Spiritual Coach, and Certified Life Coach of Pray the Impossible, I will provide you with skills, tools, techniques, and godly wisdom to help you navigate life's situations that seem impossible to get through.

Navigate:

Plan and direct the route or course of a ship, aircraft, or other form of transportation, especially by using instruments or maps.

Travel on a desired course after planning a route.

Impossible:

incapable of being or of occurring felt to be incapable of being done, attained, or fulfilled; insuperably difficult

I would define Navigating the Impossible as:

Traveling on a course using tools to help you on your journey, which is felt to be incapable of being navigated, after planning a direct course.

» To move forward, you'll need to be clear about what you want, be aware of all your options, know that there's no room for limiting beliefs, and have a solid plan of action.

» Get focused on what you really want in this next phase of your life.

» Engage with this loss/crisis/situation/life-changing event and define who you want to be. What happened to us does not define who we are.

- Identify your values and how you can effectively express them.
- Create a vision for life after the transition.
- Develop strategies to navigate the transition with ease.
- Clarify a new direction and take the necessary steps to make it happen.

CHAPTER 16

NAVIGATE

THE IMPOSSIBLE WORKBOOK

Familiar Key Life Issues

- » I do not know how to navigate through a crisis, change, or transition.
- » This is my first experience with a death of someone close to me.
- » I have encountered a major loss.
- » I am unable to see the light at the end of the tunnel.
- » I feel hopeless.
- » Stress and anxiety paralyze me.
- » I struggle with adjusting my life due to my loss.
- » I want to have more joy in my life.
- » I do not know, understand, or comprehend the purpose of the pain.
- » I feel perplexed, going through the motions in day-to-day activities.

Transitions are a natural part of life and can be challenging for most people. Answering and engaging in the questions in the next section will help you to move forward, be clear about what's been your biggest challenge, and shift your focus about your next phase of life.

I do not know how to navigate through a crisis, change, or transition.

1. What is the crisis, change, or transition that you are currently experiencing?
2. Describe in detail how it has made you feel.
3. What is difficult about these life changes?
4. How is the crisis, change, or transition affecting you?
5. What steps can you take to move forward?

This is my first experience with a death of someone close to me.

1. Who is the loved one who passed?
2. How did you feel when you heard of their passing?
3. How was your relationship with them at the time of their passing?
4. What are some happy memories you have of them?
5. Can you use your spirituality to help with your grieving and mourning?

I have encountered a major loss.

1. What is the major loss that you experienced?
2. How does this loss make you feel?
3. Do you view this loss as a setback? If so, explain.
4. What part of the loss are you struggling with?
5. Do you believe that with loss, there is a purposeful gain?

I am unable to see the light at the end of the tunnel.

1. Are you experiencing, or have you experienced, adversity or hardship for a long period of time? If so, please describe the experience.
2. Have your circumstances, situations, and despair created a mentality that things will never get better?
3. Do you feel like giving up? If so, what challenge is causing you to feel that way?
4. What about your situation leads you to believe there will not be light at the end of the tunnel?
5. What can you learn from this to use as motivation to keep going?

I feel hopeless.

1. When things are going great, what is your source of hope?
2. What life event onset the feeling of hopelessness? Describe in detail.
3. What about the incident is causing you to feel hopeless?
4. Do you believe that things will get better?
5. What steps can you take to tap back into your source of hope?

Stress and anxiety paralyze me.

1. What is currently causing your stress and anxiety?
2. What activities, thoughts, or situations usually trigger stress and anxiety for you?
3. What about stress and anxiety causes you to become paralyzed? Describe how this makes you feel.
4. What coping mechanism or techniques do you use to reduce stress and anxiety?
5. How can you move through stress and anxiety without allowing the paralysis to take over?

I struggle with making adjustments to my life due to my loss.

1. What about the loss is causing you to struggle with making changes?
2. Are you uncertain about what's next for your life after the loss?
3. What adjustments do you need to make, and will they enhance your life?
4. Has the loss left an impression that life will not get better? If so, explain in detail.
5. Have you faced and addressed the feelings that are hindering you from adjusting?

I want to have more joy in my life.

1. What are you experiencing that has stolen your joy?
2. What does joy look like?
3. What can you do to create more joy in your life?
4. What are you doing now to bring joy into your life?
5. What brings you the most fulfillment in life?

I do not know, understand, or comprehend the purpose for the pain.

1. Have you asked, "Why did this happen to me?" If so, what do you think the answer is?
2. Do you believe the pain is meant to push you into purpose for something greater than you know?
3. Could this pain be revealing things about you that you've suppressed?
4. How can you turn this pain into something purposeful to help others?
5. What can you learn from the pain?

I feel perplexed, going through the motions in day-to-day activities.

1. What part of your situation has you perplexed?
2. How is this feeling affecting your life?
3. Are you willing to try something different to break the cycle?
4. Describe your daily routine and how it makes you feel.
5. What intentional steps can you take to shift your feelings, energy, and attitude?

GETTING TO KNOW YOU

Below, write words that describe who you were in the past before the loss, describe who you are now since the loss, and describe who you want to become after the loss. For example: Happy, Sad, Lost, Depressed.

In order for the impossible to be navigated, you have to start at the beginning, then focus on where you are now, and then see where you want to go.

Write a letter from your future self to your present self. Share all the things that you have accomplished, all the things that you have worked through, and how you turned your greatest loss into a purposeful win. (At the end of the year, revisit this letter to see what became possible.)

NAVIGATE THE IMPOSSIBLE ACTIVITY

Navigating the Impossible: Traveling on a course using tools to help you on your journey, which is felt to be incapable of being navigated, after planning a direct course.

Navigate the Impossible: What are some things that you've been experiencing that have changed the course of your life?

Face the Impossible: Write down things you've been struggling with that have hindered you from moving forward in life.

Do the Impossible: Write down what you're willing to do to get unstuck and heal, and how you will use your experience for greater purpose.

____

____

____

____

____

____

____

____

____

____

____

____

____

____

____

NAVIGATE THE IMPOSSIBLE FLIP THE SWITCH ACTIVITY

When we shift our thoughts, we shift our perspective. Write down what you believe is impossible, and then write down ways that it can become possible.

____

____

____

____

____

____

____

____

____

____

____

____

____

Now that you have spent time analyzing, reflecting, and answering the questions, it's time to get focused on what you really want in this next phase of your life. Is it healing, peace, forgiveness, joy, love, happiness, experiencing new life after death, or to live in and with purpose? This is your opportunity to engage with the loss and define who you want to be, what you're going to heal, and how you're going to move forward in life. With loss comes the chance to create a vision, develop strategies, and clarify a new direction in turning your greatest loss into a purposeful win.

Brandi J-E McAlister, MS, CSC, CLC is a New Jersey native. She obtained her BA in Mass Communications from Virginia State University. Later, she completed her MS in Integrated Marketing Communication from Manhattanville College. Her passion for encouraging and helping others led her to Life Purpose Institute, where she acquired her certifications as a

Certified Spiritual Coach and Certified Life Coach. She is a member of the illustrious Delta Sigma Theta Sorority, Inc.

Brandi is an award-winning author of the Devotional of the Year titled *Real Talk: A Conversation From My Heart to Yours* and Amazon's #1 New Release titled *My Way or God's Will? The Choice is Yours*. She is the self-proclaimed Spiritual Friendvisor of Pray the Impossible. She defines Spiritual Friendvisor as a friend who gives advice based on godly wisdom. She drops daily GEMS (God Enthused Messages Spoken) from her heart based on godly wisdom.

Through her spiritual journey, she stands by her life motto, "Impacting lives one conversation at a time."

As the founder of Blessed by Brandi, Inc., a 501c3 nonprofit organization, her mission is to address the whole person by tapping into the mind, body, and spirit to get to the root of one's issues that have had the greatest impact on their spirituality, well-being, mental health, and physical health.

She learned through her transformation that God chose her for this unique assignment because she's relatable; she is what this generation needs to see and experience God in a new way. She prides herself on showing others that they can be authentic, walk in their purpose, live life to the fullest, turn up, and still love and serve God in the unique way He's called them.

www.ingramcontent.com/pod-product-compliance
Lightning Source LLC
LaVergne TN
LVHW020642100826
845148LV00012B/2299
* 9 7 9 8 9 8 6 4 6 4 2 8 2 *